HOPI

Big Buddy Books
An Imprint of Abdo Publishing
www.abdopublishing.com

Sarah Tieck

www.abdopublishing.com

Published by Abdo Publishing, a division of ABDO, PO Box 398166, Minneapolis, Minnesota 55439.
Copyright © 2015 by Abdo Consulting Group, Inc. International copyrights reserved in all countries. No part
of this book may be reproduced in any form without written permission from the publisher. Big Buddy Books™
is a trademark and logo of Abdo Publishing.

Printed in the United States of America, North Mankato, Minnesota.
102014
012015

Cover Photo: *Getty Images*: Dave Etheridge-Barnes/Contributor; Shutterstock.com.
Interior Photos: ASSOCIATED PRESS (pp. 27, 30); © Mark Burnett/Alamy (p. 25); *Getty Images*: American School
    (p. 17), John Cancalosi (pp. 5, 29), Evans/Stringer (p. 23); © NativeStock.com/Angel Wynn (pp. 9, 11, 13, 15, 17,
    21, 26); © North Wind Picture Archives (p. 9); © M. Timothy O'Keefe/Alamy (p. 16); Shutterstock.com (p. 19).

Coordinating Series Editor: Rochelle Baltzer
Contributing Editors: Megan M. Gunderson, Marcia Zappa
Graphic Design: Adam Craven

Library of Congress Cataloging-in-Publication Data

Tieck, Sarah, 1976-
  Hopi / Sarah Tieck.
    pages cm. -- (Native Americans)
  ISBN 978-1-62403-580-7
  1. Hopi Indians--Juvenile literature. I. Title.
  E99.H7T47 2015
  979.1004'97458--dc23
                          2014028399

CONTENTS

Amazing People

Hundreds of years ago, North America was mostly wild, open land. Native American tribes lived on the land. They had their own languages and **customs**.

The Hopi (HOH-pee) are one Native American tribe. They are known for their religious beliefs and weaving skills. Let's learn more about these Native Americans.

Did You Know?

The name *Hopi* means "peaceful ones."

Hopi social dances are often open to the public. Tribe members dress in traditional clothing and makeup to perform them.

Hopi Territory

Hopi homelands were in the American Southwest. The tribe lived in what is now northeastern Arizona. The Hopi are connected to the Pueblo people. They are considered the westernmost Pueblo tribe.

HOPI NATION TODAY

CANADA

UNITED STATES

UTAH

COLORADO

ARIZONA

NEW MEXICO

MEXICO

N
W E
S

HOME LIFE

Most Hopi families lived in homes made of stone and **adobe**. These were built on **mesas**. They had several levels and many rooms.

Usually, a home had a rooftop entrance. People climbed down a ladder through a hole in the ceiling. There were ground floor rooms without doors. These were used for storage.

 Village squares had underground rooms called kivas. Religious ceremonies were often held in them.

 The Hopi used ladders to move between levels in their homes.

What They Ate

The Hopi were skilled farmers. They grew vegetables, such as beans and squash. And they planted fruits, including melons.

The Hopi also farmed corn, or maize. They used special stones to grind corn into cornmeal.

In addition to farming, Hopi women gathered berries, nuts, and seeds. The men hunted rabbit, elk, antelope, and deer.

Growing food was a major part of Hopi life.

Daily Life

The Hopi lived in towns. A man would move in with his wife's family. Several families would live together in a group.

The Hopi wore moccasins. Women wore dresses made from cloth woven by the men. Men wore simple cloths to cover their lower bodies. Men and women used woven blankets to stay warm.

 Women wore manta dresses for special events. Patterns and colors changed based on the event.

In a Hopi town, people had different jobs. Men farmed plants and herded animals. They were builders, hunters, weavers, and chiefs.

Women took care of the children and ran the homes. They got water and made food, such as cornmeal.

Children learned by helping and watching others in the community. They became part of religious **ceremonies** around age six.

Some Hopi men still weave cloth. They use upright looms to create a tight weave.

Made by Hand

The Hopi made many objects by hand. They often used natural materials. These arts and crafts added beauty to everyday life.

Woven Cloth

Hopi men were talented weavers. They spun cotton or wool into thread. Then they wove that into cloth. The cloth was used to make blankets and clothing.

Moccasins

Hopi men made moccasins from deerskin. Hopi moccasins had soles that came up around the sides of the foot. Ties or a silver button held them closed. Some moccasins were decorated for special occasions.

Kachina Dolls

Kachina dolls were carved from wood. They were decorated with masks, headdresses, and clothing. These dolls stood for spirits. They were often given to children but were not toys.

Pottery

Hopi pottery was used in daily life. Many pieces were considered works of art. Hopi pottery is known for strong colors and patterns. Some pots took hours to create.

Spirit Life

The Hopi believed in many gods and spirits. These included Earth Mother and Sky Father. Kachinas were other important spirits.

The Hopi observed **ceremonies** and **rituals**. These were meant to keep the world balanced and the Hopi safe. Sometimes, the Hopi performed kachina dances wearing masks and costumes.

Did You Know?

Soyal was a ceremony held in December on the shortest day of the year. The Hopi prayed and planned for the year to come.

The Hopi consider the Grand Canyon the *sipapu*. This means the place where they came into this world.

STORYTELLERS

Stories are important to the Hopi. The best storytellers are called *tuwutsmoki*. They collect and remember stories to share Hopi **culture** and history. They begin by saying whether a story is true or not.

The Hopi tell stories about how they came into the world. Spider Woman is a character who appears in the Hopi creation story. Hopi stories are also about kachinas.

Did You Know?

The Hopi speak a unique language. They have different ways of describing time.

The Hopi say the word *aliksa'i* to tell listeners that a story is starting.

FIGHTING FOR LAND

The first Hopi villages were built before 1200. The Hopi were related to the Pueblo people, but they had their own way of life.

In 1540, the Spanish arrived in Hopi territory. They explored and searched for gold. They brought over sheep. By the 1600s, they started to build **missions** on Hopi land. They changed the Hopi way of life. For example, the Hopi started herding sheep.

Sheep became important to the Hopi way of life. The Hopi spent many hours caring for their herds.

The Hopi struggled after the Spanish arrived. Many died from European sicknesses. Later, they suffered hunger, more illness, and problems with crops.

Land was important to the Hopi. In 1882, the US government placed the Hopi **reservation** within the Navajo reservation. For many years, the two tribes battled for control of land. The Hopi continue to **protect** their land and way of life.

As a federally recognized tribe, the Hopi have their own police and government.

BACK IN TIME

1540

The Hopi met Spanish explorers for the first time.

About 1150

The village of Oraibi was founded by the Hopi. It is one of the oldest US settlements that people still live in.

1882

The US government set up a Hopi **reservation**. This was surrounded by Navajo land. For many years, the Navajo and Hopi fought each other for land.

1887

A school for Hopi children opened in Kearns Canyon, Arizona. It was set up to help them learn English and American ways. Some Hopi did not want this.

1936

The Hopi set up their Tribal Council and government.

1974

The Navajo-Hopi Land Settlement Act was passed. It returned 900,000 acres (360,000 ha) of Navajo lands to the Hopi.

THE HOPI TODAY

The Hopi have a long, rich history. They are remembered for their colorful clothing and religious **ceremonies**.

Hopi roots run deep. Today, the people have kept alive those special things that make them Hopi. Even though times have changed, many people carry the **traditions**, stories, and memories of the past into the present.

Did You Know?

Today, there are about 15,000 Hopi in the United States.

The Hopi keep many of their traditions alive today.

"Our goals are not to gain political control, monetary wealth, nor military power but rather to pray and to promote the welfare of all living beings and to preserve the world in a natural way."

— Thomas Banyacya, Hopi traditional elder

GLOSSARY

adobe (uh-DOH-bee) a type of brick or building material made from sun-dried earth and straw.

ceremony a formal event on a special occasion.

culture (KUHL-chuhr) the arts, beliefs, and ways of life of a group of people.

custom a practice that has been around a long time and is common to a group or a place.

mesa (MAY-suh) a hill with a flat top and steep sides.

mission a place where religious work is done.

protect (pruh-TEHKT) to guard against harm or danger.

reservation (reh-zuhr-VAY-shuhn) a piece of land set aside by the government for Native Americans to live on.

ritual (RIH-chuh-wuhl) a formal act or set of acts that is repeated.

tradition (truh-DIH-shuhn) a belief, a custom, or a story handed down from older people to younger people.

WEBSITES

To learn more about Native Americans, visit **booklinks.abdopublishing.com**. These links are routinely monitored and updated to provide the most current information available.

INDEX